The Freedom of Naturism

A Guide for the How and Why of Adopting a Naturist Lifestyle

by Augustine Rae

Table of Contents

Introduction

Another word for "naturism" is "nudism," which should be rather self-explanatory. Due to Judeo-Christian-Islamic influence, however, there are a lot of negative connotations associated with it. Despite the separation of church and state (at least in the West), religious sensibilities still play a very powerful influence over civil law, which is why you can be arrested for being naked in public.

Even the irreligious, as well as those of an atheistic bent, have been conditioned to think of nudity as being something wrong. It is associated with vulnerability and shame at best, or with sexuality and arousal at worst.

The Torah, the Bible, and the Koran all agree that Adam and Eve ate of the apple of knowledge in disobedience of god's law. And what did they learn? The first thing they learned was the difference between good and evil. The second thing they learned was that they were naked. And thus was born the fashion industry.

Throw in Christian and Muslim missionaries spreading their ideas all over the world, often through force and genocide, and well... the rest is history. But at least they committed

1

their atrocities while modestly dressed, so they couldn't have been that bad.

The problem with modesty has to do with the fact that different cultures define, understand, and express it in very different ways.

In Papua New Guinea, for example, some tribes have their men walk about butt naked by our standards, save for penis gourds that leave their balls hanging. In some Philippine tribes, women define modesty by covering themselves from their waists to their ankles, and never mind the rest. Until recently, the Waorani women of Ecuador signified modesty by tying a string around their waists, and that was about it.

Naturism is antithetical to all of these. It does not seek to conform to any societal definitions of modesty — quite the opposite, in fact. It believes that going about naked (sans penis gourds, sarongs, and waist strings) whenever possible, is the ideal condition because it's natural, hence its name.

It also feels incredibly good!

This book will introduce naturism and explain why it's not the same thing as nudity. It will also discuss the psychology from an insider's point of view and why it's such a great thing to do, challenge your ideas and misconceptions about nudity, as well as dispel several myths about it.

Resources will also be provided should you wish to explore this practice further, or to embrace it completely by diving off the deep end.

Chapter 1: Naturism versus Nudism

In America, naturism and nudism are synonymous. In Britain and some other European countries, however, they are very different things.

To the Brits, nudism is simply about being naked, while naturism is a way of life dictated by certain values and practices. Recently, however, a growing number of Americans have also begun making a similar distinction, thanks the growing influence of organizations like the International Naturist Federation.

So what sets a nudist apart from someone who's simply taken their clothes off? A nudist is one who prefers doing without clothing whenever and wherever possible. It is important to understand that while some get a sexual thrill from this, that's not what nudism is all about. Those who get off (pardon the pun) on being naked are generally exhibitionists and thrill seekers, but we have no room to get into detail about that here.

Nudists are people who are simply more comfortable being naked. They prefer walking or lounging about, doing chores or simply relaxing, as well as sleeping in the buff. There's no chafing, no sweat-soaked clothes that stick to the body, and no discomfort, whatsoever; the weather allowing, of course.

Those who enjoy skinny dipping qualify as nudists, by the way, but care must be taken when using this word. In many parts of the non-English world, a number of cultures actually consider it normal to swim or bathe in the nude.

In Japan, for example, group bathing in public bath houses is the norm. In certain communities, men and women even bathe together. Whether it is a unisex bath house or a mixed one, it is considered extremely rude to enter the water with clothing on — except for a towel you put on your head, that is. In the Japanese cultural context, these people are not nudists, they are simply being practical and respectful of everyone.

This attitude applies to many German speaking regions of Europe, as well as to several Scandinavian countries. There, people generally enter saunas in the nude, then go dipping into a lake or pool to cool off, also in the nude. Entire families engage in this practice with no thought that what they are doing is strange, improper, or immoral.

While the Japanese and the northern European peoples wouldn't dream of going nude in public, they generally see nothing wrong with it in certain venues and at certain times. Most of these people would not consider themselves nudists. They simply see themselves as obeying certain traditions, customs, and norms.

In these cases, nudity is not associated with sexuality or even sexual arousal. It is simply expected of everyone, so to do otherwise would be considered inappropriate.

Naturists, on the other hand, live according to a certain creed. They not only see nudity as the appropriate way that people should be, they also see it as an ethical and healthy way to live.

As far as naturists are concerned, clothing should only be used for protection in certain seasons and for certain jobs. Where appropriate, they also see clothes as being fine for certain ceremonial functions. Think of the wearing of a suit or a uniform. While these are appropriate at work, in school, or in church, they are not appropriate at home or in other leisurely settings.

This is because naturist philosophy is egalitarian in nature. As such, it teaches that clothes are divisive in nature and inherently wrong. When not used as a bulwark against the weather and as protection in certain professions or activities (like frying food), clothes keep people apart.

Sounds strange? Think about it. Clothes define people's religious, cultural, and ethnic identities. Examples of this include the headscarves worn by some Muslim women, the turbans worn by Sikh men, or the Stetson hats worn by some in the American south.

Clothes also reflect socio-economic status, separating the haves from the have-nots; think of Giorgio Armani versus cheap Chinese fake knock-offs. In the work force, they are sometimes used to denote hierarchy — especially the differences between blue collar and white collar workers, or between supervisors and underlings.

Naturists also believe that nudity is the default human condition. They argue that clothes are a manmade invention and that our ancestors managed without them long before the discovery of fur, leather, and fabric. They also cite the health benefits of the sun (in moderation and with protective creams) and of exposure to the elements.

From an ecological perspective, clothes generate an industry of waste. What's hip today won't be so tomorrow, forcing people to buy new fashions in order to remain proper and up-to-date. One must also consider the expense involved in cleaning, as well as the amount of chemicals and water used.

To naturists, those who prefer to wear clothes all the time, even when it's not necessary (such as in the privacy of the home), are called textilists.

While nudists simply prefer being naked, naturists embrace an entire culture and lifestyle. The latter generally promote ecological practices and healthy living. A number also encourage the practice of yoga, vegetarianism, and alternative forms of medicine, though not necessarily all at the same time.

In short, anyone can be a nudist, but not everyone is cut out to be a naturist or even wants to be one. The former is a preference, while the latter is a philosophy.

Chapter 2: The Different Types of Nudists

The word "naturism" was first coined in 1778 by Jean Baptiste Luc Planchon, a Belgian physician, who described it as "the natural style of life and health." As such, the movement has had enough time to diversify.

1) Individual nudists

Are those who are only comfortable with nudity when alone, though they are not averse to being so with someone they are intimate with. They have no social, philosophical, political, or economic agenda; only that they're more comfortable being naked whenever possible, but away from prying eyes.

2) Family nudists

Are those who are comfortable being nude only with family members, but who would be uncomfortable being in the same state with strangers or those they are not familiar with. A number of Germanic, Scandinavian, Japanese, and other cultural groups fall under this category.

Among such people, nudity is acceptable in the home and under certain circumstances, but is frowned upon at other times. These do not generally consider themselves to be nudists, however.

3) Wilderness nudists

Are those who go nude only in rural, out of the way places. Some go camping specifically so they can get naked, preferring to avoid nudist or naturist camps. Still others do so as part of a ritual, such as some followers of the Wiccan religion. While some consider themselves to be nudists, others (such as Wiccans) do not, seeing nudity merely as part of a necessary rite.

4) Social nudists

Are those who visit each other's homes to be nude in a social setting, or visit nudist or naturist camps on a regular basis. There are a growing number of such venues worldwide, which will be covered later.

5) Militant naturists

Are the hardcore followers of naturism. These tend to live either part time or exclusively in naturist camps. A number actively campaign to legalize public nudity, as well as other agendas they believe in, such as environmentalism, yoga, alternative health, or socialism — or at least greater government regulation over capitalism, which they see as inherently destructive.

These naturists tend to look down on nudists, whom they see as either wannabes at best, or closet exhibitionists who hide behind the cloak of naturism at worst. Some militant naturists complain that nudists benefit from the campaigning they have done.

6) Spiritual nudists

These are generally exclusive to Indian holy men, such as the Hindu naga sadhus and the Jain digambars. Naga sadhus are usually attached to the sect of Shiva, the destroyer god of the Hindu pantheon who allegedly taught yoga, dance, and music to humanity. Since Shiva was traditionally depicted as being naked, the naga sadhus also go about naked in an attempt to identify with their patron deity.

Although the Jain religion opens monkhood up to both genders, only qualified men go about naked, though not all do. Since Mahavir, the founder of Jainism, went about in the nude to show he had no attachments to the material world, whatsoever, digambars do the same.

It is not uncommon to see such naked men throughout India. Some even go on national television to give religious lectures. Indians of all religions view their nudity as a form of spiritual practice, an extreme form of ascetism which inspires others to lead a moral life and turn away from materialism.

Please note, however, that nudists, like everyone else, are complex. With the exception of naga sadhus and digambars, most are not exclusively one or the other. Since the dividing line between a nudist and a naturist is not always clear, and varies from one place to another, most fall under several categories depending on the situation.

As such, an individual nudist might visit a naturist camp and become a social one, while a family nudist might think nothing of going out camping over the holidays and leaving all their clothes behind in the car.

Again with the exception of naga sadhus and digambars, nudists do not practice their way of life 24-7. Even those who live full time in naturist communities, such as the village of Camp d'Agde in France, find themselves having to wear clothing when appropriate.

These people understand that they are the minority and have to function in a predominantly textilist world. As such, many hold on to their clothes and wear them when it is required of them.

Even militant naturists wear clothes, especially when they campaign for certain laws. As such, however, they tend to get really antsy when textilists enter their territories while dressed. Naturists and nudists are people who therefore live in two worlds simultaneously.

Chapter 3: Common Misconceptions about Naturism

Thanks to religion, culture, the media, and outright ignorance, there are so many misconceptions about nudity. While Western classical art appreciates the nude in paintings and sculpture, and accepts that people in pre-Christian Europe thought nothing of the practice, modern people are expected to be more enlightened and act accordingly. Bearing in mind that people are unique and that there are exceptions to everything, most nudists and naturists complain about the following myths:

1) Nudist and naturist venues are places where people have sex

Most such places have strict policies in place which put a ban on public sex, photography, and outright exhibitionism — especially since many are open to families complete with grandparents and children. Outright voyeurism is therefore prohibited in many places, such as the banning of cameras. Violators are often expelled, blacklisted, and prosecuted. While sex is not prohibited in these places, per se, it cannot be public.

2) Nudist and naturist venues are sexually stimulating places

Virtually everyone who's gone to such a venue finds the truth to be disappointingly otherwise. When everyone around you: men, women, children, the young and the old, are naked, sex is often the last thing to come to mind. Within a day or two, most forget that they and everyone else around them are nude.

It's called conditioning, as well as social acclimatization. Wearing a Frankenstein outfit may make you stand out at any other time of the year, but when Halloween comes around, chances are that you'll blend right in with everyone else. In a strictly nudist setting, it's the clothed person who stands out and gets stared at.

Sexual arousal as a result of visual cues is a cultural construct, the product of social conditioning. Among the Surma and Mursi peoples of Ethiopia, for example, women pull out their lower teeth then slit their lower lips in order to accommodate lip plates, which their men find hot.

It's all about what everyone around you does and what you get used to. Some Arab men who are used to seeing women covered in full burqa become overly heated at the sight of women whose faces, arms, and legs are exposed. For those of us used to such things, it's generally no big deal.

Many find that it's clothing that's sexually stimulating, or at least, various states of undress. When nothing is left to the imagination, however, the fire surprisingly tends to die out.

3) Only those with great bodies go to nudist and naturist camps

Nudist camps which only grant admission to good-looking people with great bodies are often swinger organizations or gay-only venues. They do exist, but cannot be considered naturist, as exclusivity violates the egalitarian philosophy of naturism.

Naturist venues are open to everyone: men and women, young and old, the beautiful and the otherwise. Even those who want to go to these places often stay away because they feel insecure about their bodies.

These insecurities are exactly what naturism seeks to address, among others. It teaches that textilists are inherently judgmental and shallow because of clothing. Clothing is an artificial construct, subject to fashion, culture, religion, and even politics. As such, people are taught to judge others by how they look and by how well they try to fit in or not.

Naturists believe that because nature is diverse, so people come in all shapes and sizes. To judge others by how they look, therefore, is to go against the natural order. It teaches people to look only at the exterior while ignoring the interior. As far as some naturists are concerned, this is one of the many reasons why misunderstanding, racism, class division, and conflicts occur.

All naturist camps have their share of fat and skinny, old and young, muscular and otherwise. It is not about exhibitionism — which naturists condemn. It is about accepting who you are, regardless of your imperfections, as well as accepting others for the same. Naturism is about simply being, it is not about beauty contests — which naturists abhor.

4) Naturists are immoral people

No doubt there are some who have few scruples, but naturism itself is devoted to ethical principles. It believes in being open-minded and in accepting people for who they are regardless of their race, religion, sexuality, profession, or political beliefs.

Naturism is also devoted to the ecology and to the practice of conservation. A number live full time in naturist camps which try to be self-sustaining, make use of alternative fuels, and even grow their own organic food. Many also believe in living simply by avoiding the excesses of consumerism.

5) Naturists and nudists are pedophiles

Since a number of these venues are family-oriented, many believe that children become sexualized at a young age. Registered nudist and naturist venues for families have strict rules that only allow children in if they are accompanied by their families. Where children are not yet potty-trained, they are required to wear diapers. Also, families keep an eye out for each other's children, as do the camp organizers. Nudist camps for swingers and gay-only venues, however, have a strict adults-only policy.

Chapter 4: Children and Nudity

This is perhaps the biggest problem textilists have with naturists. With all the pedophilic scandals out there, many believe that children who grow up in naturist communities or with naturist parents become sexualized at a young age. Some have even argued that children who grow up in such a setting are victims and that their parents' rights over them should therefore be terminated.

Such accusations have prompted official studies into the matter, both here in America, as well as in Europe. There are a number of these studies available, so feel free to look them up on your own.

The studies found that there is no correlation between pedophilia and nudity in the home. In fact, the sexualization of children is higher in more conservative, textilist families than in nudist or naturist ones.

Studies of cultures where social nudity is the norm, or where social nudity is considered acceptable in certain situations, reinforces such claims. It's all about what people grow up with and get used to. Remember: naturism and naturist groups have been around for centuries. Before them, there was pre-Christian Europe and the pre-Islamic Middle East.

Naturists complain, and rightly so, that textilists seek to impose their own values on others with the same missionary zeal that the early Christians imposed their beliefs upon formerly non-Christian cultures.

On the topic of Christianity, a number accuse the Catholic Church of hypocrisy on the subject of pedophilia for reasons we need not get into, on the assumption you've not been living under a rock. Others point to children's beauty pageants, where prepubescent girls get dolled up and paraded before the public as the sexualization of children. There are also cultures where nudity is considered shameful, but who think nothing of marrying off their sexually immature daughters to older men.

Based on these and other examples, naturists argue that it is not group nudity that causes pedophilia or the sexualization of minors. Most victims of sexual abuse grow up in textilist homes, after all. Aside from some cultural norms, such as those which encourage child marriages, the causes of pedophilia are complex and clearly not the result of either textilist or naturist lifestyles.

It can be said, therefore, that a state of undress does not sexualize either adults or children. As of this writing, no naturist has yet lost their parental rights in any country due to their lifestyle. Textilists who accuse naturists of pedophilia are not only hypocrites, they also reveal their own insecurities and repressed fantasies.

Chapter 5: Naturist Ideals

While naturists are a diverse lot, the centuries have provided them with a vast body of literature by which to create certain common traditions. It cannot be emphasized enough, however, that different groups practice or emphasize certain things over others, while some take a more laissez-faire attitude toward the philosophy.

1) Nudity is natural

Nudity is the default human condition. Being naked, especially when outside, allows people to develop a greater rapport with nature. It also reawakens the human body to sensations that have become dulled through years of being covered up, making people more in tune to their body's wisdom.

2) Nudity is healthy

Many naturists claim that being naked, especially in nature, has healing benefits, and that it can strengthen the human body against disease. Ayurveda (traditional Indian medicine) even recommends the exposure of the chest as a means of toughening the body up, though it does not encourage genital exposure. Increased exposure to sunlight (in moderation) also increases the intake of Vitamin D which combats osteoporosis, diabetes, heart disease, and some forms of cancer.

In Europe, many pediatricians recommend letting infants have regular doses of nude time in order to allow them a full range of motion. The reasoning behind this is that allowing infants free movement stimulates neuron growth, which contributes to brain development and cognitive function. Admittedly, there are those who argue that modern diapers in no way hampers full movement. The naturist counter-argument will follow.

Others argue that clothing provides fertile breeding grounds for fungi and bacteria, which can result in body odor, yeast infections, athlete's foot, and even urinary tract infections. There's also the problem with deer ticks that latch onto thick fabric, and when they bite, can result in Lyme disease. Sea lice also have a nasty tendency of latching onto the crotches of bathing suits.

Tight belts, ties, and girdles can impede breathing. For men, tight pants increase testicular temperature, which lowers sperm count and reduces fertility. Surely there's no need to get into the problems caused by tight shoes and high heels?

On the topic of footwear, have you visited a pediatrician, lately? They're now recommending going barefoot. It's been found that going barefoot stimulates your brain into growing extra neural connections, which can prevent Alzheimer's, boost memory, and improve cognitive ability.

3) Nudity promotes sanity

Many social nudists claim that they have less hang ups about their bodies and are more accepting of their physical shortcomings. They also believe that their lifestyle encourages a sincere respect for the opposite gender, while others claim that it reduces porn addiction.

4) Nudity promotes equality

This was discussed earlier. Without clothes, people have little else by which to connote social and economic status. Also, it becomes harder to denote religious, cultural, and political affiliations. As to one's racial background, naturists argue that skin color and body hair aside, people tend to be pretty similar from the neck down.

5) Nudity encourages honesty

Naturists believe that clothing promotes dishonesty and encourages hypocrisy. They insist that one of the reasons people become superficial is because they can hide behind clothes which can be tailored to make them seem other than what they are.

6) Nudity is about simplicity

Though not all naturists are on board with this, many are, citing a number of naturist writers, such as Walt Whitman and Henry David Thoreau (yes, they were naturists!). The idea behind this is that nudity is not enough; one should also strip one's life to the barest necessities for comfort and survival.

While some naturists practice a vegetarian lifestyle, not all do. Most, however, believe in practicing some form of moderation, such as cutting back on alcohol and tobacco consumption, as well as meat and recreational drugs.

7) Nudity is about the environment

Naturists have a deep respect for the environment and believe that the fashion industry promotes unsustainable practices that hurt the planet. Besides the amount of material needed to sustain ever changing fashions, the fashion industry makes use of chemicals and other additives for color, texture, and cleaning.

Clothes also make their way into landfills. Artificial fabrics like nylon and rayon, while biodegradable, take decades to decay completely, another environmental no-no.

As to the baby diaper industry, this too has come under fire, since a number are made of non-biodegradable material that ends up in landfills. Diaper rash is another problem for some. Those who do use diapers tend to resort to the traditional cloth-and-pin type which can be washed and reused.

Chapter 6: Naturist Etiquette

There are certain forms of etiquette that most naturist camps require you to observe.

1) Find out what you're getting into

Many believe that naturist camps are new. They're not. Some families have been naturist for generations and have therefore developed certain rules and traditions they expect all visitors to adhere to. Since most established venues have a website, visit it first and call to make sure you know what their requirements are.

2) Most require an invitation

Most naturist camps are small, so they only have limited facilities that can only accommodate a certain number of people. Before you visit one, it's best to secure an invitation first and to reserve accommodations.

In Europe, invitations are rarely needed, but a number in North America do require it. If this cannot be secured by knowing an actual naturist who's a member of a camp or organization, it can be had by calling the facility in advance.

3) Don't be too curious

Some people are new and are still getting their bearings. These prefer not to give out details about themselves, so if someone gives out just their first name, don't insist on getting their last names, as well. Respect their privacy and chosen boundaries.

4) No staring

Staring at people's faces is fine. Doing so with other parts of their anatomy is rude. Also, don't make comments about people's figures. That aside, most people really do get over the nudity thing within a few hours of being in a social gathering of naturists. After a while, most actually forget they're naked.

5) No cameras

Every single nudist and naturist camp has a strict no-pictures policy. Those who bring cameras to a site are required to leave them with the front desk, which will relinquish them when you leave.

6) No exhibitionism

Kissing, hugging, and other forms of physical affection are considered fine, but don't get too carried away, at least not in front of others. Most naturist camps are family oriented, so you should be mindful of children. Some even have a strict no-swearing policy in place.

Where men are concerned, erections must be kept hidden. This can easily be achieved by sitting cross-legged, covering it with a towel, getting into the water, or avoiding sexually stimulating conversations. Many accredited sites also ban pornographic material or literature.

7) Clothing

This is allowed when cooking. Those with toddlers are required to put diapers on them so as to keep the facilities as clean as possible.

In places which border textilist sites, such as beaches, visitors are asked to bring along towels or trunks they can hop into in the event they cross over into textilist territory. This allows them to avoid causing upset or facing potential arrest.

In such cases, however, there are always boundary markers and signs which warn textilists to expect nudists. Where these are legal, such as states like Florida, police are not allowed to arrest nudists, so long as they do not actually infringe upon textilist areas. In other words, even if you are visibly naked to others, so long as you remain on official nudist soil, the law cannot and will not prosecute you.

Chapter 7:   Naturist Groups and Associations

The International Naturist Federation is the largest naturist organization and has a vast, directory that'll help you get in touch with people, organizations, and facilities around the world. Please note that the INF is not in charge of most of the groups and camps that are affiliated with it, as most of those are independent. Rather, it provides a venue where naturists can meet and liaise with each other. Membership does come with benefits, however, which you might want to check out.

If you're in the United States, a good place to get started is with the American Association for Nude Recreation. It used to be affiliated with the INF, but withdrew its membership in 2010. Though devoted to recreation, the AANR is also political, and has lobbied the US and Canadian governments for nudist rights.

Another organization for Americans and Canadians is the Naturist Society. They boast several member sites throughout North America and provide online and magazine subscriptions for members to keep in touch with the world of nudity/naturism. If you live outside North America, you can find a directory of naturist organizations here: http://www.naturistplace.com/nudewrld.htm

The list given cannot be considered comprehensive by any means, but it does provide a good start. They were chosen because of their accreditation, reputation, and the fact that they are open to all.

There are nudist groups that are exclusively oriented towards specific religious (there are actually Christian nudist camps out there), racial, sexual, and age-oriented categories. As such, however, they cannot qualify as being naturist in any way.

Conclusion

In the modern Western context, naturism is considered to be an alternative lifestyle, and like all such lifestyles, is greatly misunderstood and marginalized. This is a shame, because there is so much to recommend about it.

Many who've tried it have found it to be an extremely transformative experience. It has allowed them to confront social stereotypes which they found to be completely lacking in merit. When one prejudice has been found to have no value, it isn't hard to understand how others also eventually lose their power.

Contrary to what many militant naturists claim, nudity is not the solution to all of the world's ills. It is extremely liberating, however, and how can that possibly be a bad thing?

Finally, it really does feel good.

In closing, I'd like to thank you for purchasing this book! If you enjoyed it or found it helpful, I'd greatly appreciate it if you'd take a moment to leave a review on Amazon. Thank you!

Printed in Dunstable, United Kingdom

66128860R00030